●●● BULLETPOINTS ●●●

FOOTBALL

Christopher Rigby

Miles Kelly
PUBLISHING

First published in 2004 by Miles Kelly Publishing Ltd
Bardfield Centre, Great Bardfield Essex, CM7 4SL

Copyright © 2004 Miles Kelly Publishing
Some material in this book first appeared in *1000 Things you should know*

2 4 6 8 10 9 7 5 3 1

Editor: Kate Miles

Picture Research: Liberty Newton

Design Assistant: Tom Slemmings

Production: Estela Boulton

British Library Cataloguing-in-Publication Data
A catalogue record for this book is available from the British Library

ISBN 1-84236-400-6

Printed in China

www.mileskelly.net
info@mileskelly.net

The publishers would like to thank the following artists and photographic agencies who have contributed to this book:
Janos Marffy, Mike White
Page 7 Thomas Coex/AFP/Getty Images; 8 Staff/AFP/Getty Images; 10 William West/AFP/Getty Images;
14 Adrian Dennis/AFP/Getty Images; 15 (*background*) Sony Computer Entertainment, Gerry Penny/AFP/Getty Images;
17 Cristina Quicler/AFP/Getty Images; 19 STAFF/AFP/ Getty Images; 20 Patrick Hertzog/AFP/ Getty Images;
22 Gerry Penny/AFP/Getty Images; 25 STAFF/AFP/ Getty Images; 26 STAFF/AFP/ Getty Images; 27 Paul Barker/AFP/ Getty
Images; 29 Robyn Beck/AFP/ Getty Images; 31 STAFF/AFP/ Getty Images; 33 STAFF/AFP/ Getty Images;
35 Gerard Julien/AFP/ Getty Images; 37 STAFF/AFP/ Getty Images; 39 Boris Horvat/AFP/ Getty Images

All other photographs are from : MKP archives; Corel, Digitalvision, Hemera, PhotoDisc

Contents

Origins of the game

▼ *Lads kick a ball around in a rough game of football.*

● **Early forms of football games** involving vast numbers of players were played in ancient Egypt in an attempt to till the soil to make it more fertile.

- **In England from the 11th century** onwards matches were organized between rival villages, with hundreds of players involved in violent street battles to gain possession of the ball.

- **In 1314 King Edward II banned football** from the streets of London with the threat of imprisonment for anyone who defied the ban.

- **In 1863 the London Football Association** was founded and the game became known as Association Football from which the word soccer derived.

- **The Football Association (FA)** was founded following a meeting at the Freemason's Tavern in Lincoln Inn's Field, and its first secretary was Ebenezer Cobb Morley.

- **The first set of official football rules** was published by the FA in 1863, the year of its foundation.

- **In July 1885 professional football** was legalized by the Football Association.

- **The Football League** was formed in 1888 and four years later a second division was added.

- **FIFA** was founded in 1904, the seven founder members being Switzerland, Spain, Sweden, France, Denmark, Belgium and the Netherlands.

. . . FASCINATING FACT . . .

As early as 200BC the Chinese played a game called Tsu Chu that literally means 'kick ball'.

Goalkeepers hall of fame

- **William Foulkes** – The legendary William 'Fatty' Foulkes was signed by Chelsea for £20 from Sheffield United in 1905 and tipped the scales at 152.4 kg.

- **Frank Swift** – In 1948 Frank Swift became the first goalkeeper to captain England. Ten years later he perished in the Munich air crash whilst working as a newspaper reporter.

- **Bert Trautmann** – A German soldier during World War II, he played in the 1956 FA Cup final for Manchester City in a 3–1 win against Birmingham. After the game X-rays revealed that he had broken his neck during the final.

- **Lev Yashin** – The Russian keeper is the only goalkeeper to have been voted European Footballer of the Year, an accolade he received in 1963.

- **Gordon Banks** – In 1970 Banks made what is regarded as the greatest save the world has ever seen from a goal-bound effort from the head of the legendary Pele.

- **Dino Zoff** – In 1982 Zoff became the first goalkeeper to captain a World Cup winning team, and at the age of 40 the Italian is the oldest player to win a World Cup medal.

- **Ray Clemence** – Whilst playing for Liverpool, Clemence won a host of trophies including five League championships and three European Cups. He played 61 times for England, a figure that could have trebled had it not been for Peter Shilton.

- **Peter Shilton** –
  The most capped
  England player with
  125 international caps.
  He also holds the British
  record for league appearances
  with 1005.

- **Peter Schmeichel** –
  The Great Dane was capped 128
  times for Denmark and captained
  Manchester United in their 1999
  European Cup triumph against
  Bayern Munich.

- **David Seaman** – Capped 75 times for
  England, Seaman began his career as an
  apprentice at Leeds United and went on to
  play for Peterborough, Birmingham, Queens
  Park Rangers, Arsenal and Manchester City.

▶ *The Lev Yashin Award goes
to the best goalkeeper of the
World Cup finals.*

It's a goal!

▲ *Just Fontaine (left) of France celebrates after scoring a goal past Brazilian goalkeeper Gilmar in a World Cup semifinal in 1958.*

- **In an 1885 Scottish Cup** tie Arbroath beat Bon Accord 36–0, a British record for a senior professional game that is never likely to be bettered.

- **The most goals scored** by one player in a single World Cup final is 13, a mark achieved in 1958 by Just Fontaine of France.

- **Brian Deane was the first ever player** to score in a Premiership match, when he opened the scoring for Sheffield United against Manchester United.

- **The first player to score a Premiership hat-trick** was Eric Cantona when playing for Leeds in a 5–0 win against Tottenham in 1992.

- **In the 1994/95 season** Andy Cole became the first player to score five goals in a Premiership match when Manchester United beat Ipswich 9–0, a record score for a Premiership game.

- **Only six players** have scored 30 or more goals for England. Bobby Charlton with 49, Gary Lineker with 48, Jimmy Greaves with 44 and Tom Finney, Alan Shearer and Nat Lofthouse each with 30.

- **Michael Owen** is expected to be the next player to top 30 goals for England. He scored his 24th international goal against Liechtenstein in September 2003 and many experts expect him to surpass Bobby Charlton's long-standing record.

- **In 2003** when beating Macedonia 2–1, Wayne Rooney at the age of 17 years and 317 days became England's youngest-ever goal scorer.

- **Michael Owen became the 10th player** to score 100 goals in the Premiership. His nine predecessors are Alan Shearer, Andy Cole, Les Ferdinand, Teddy Sheringham, Robbie Fowler, Dwight Yorke, Ian Wright, Dion Dublin and Matthew Le Tissier.

> **FASCINATING FACT**
> In 2001 the veteran striker Les Ferdinand scored the Premiership's 10,000th goal.

Who's the boss?

▲ *England's team coach Sven-Goran Eriksson encourages his players during a training session.*

- **Sven Goran Eriksson** is the 13th manager to take charge of England. His 12 predecessors are Kevin Keegan, Peter Taylor (caretaker), Howard Wilkinson (1 game only), Glenn Hoddle, Terry Venables, Graham Taylor, Bobby Robson, Ron Greenwood, Joe Mercer, Don Revie, Alf Ramsey and Walter Winterbottom.

- **In 1997 when Chelsea beat Middlesbrough** in the FA Cup final, Ruud Gullit became the first foreign manager to win the FA Cup.

- **Tommy Docherty once joked**, 'I've had more clubs than Jack Nicklaus'. The teams he has managed are Chelsea, QPR (twice), Rotherham, Manchester United, Aston Villa, Derby County, Preston, Wolves, Porto, Altrincham, South Melbourne and Sydney Olympic (twice).

- **Despite winning the league title with Derby County**, Brian Clough was sacked after just 44 days in charge of Leeds United. He went on to win the league title and two European Cups with Nottingham Forest.

- **At the start of the 2003/04 season** Dario Gradi was the Football League's longest-serving manager, having held the managerial reins at Crewe Alexandra since 1983.

- **Alex Ferguson** is the only manager to win European trophies with a Scottish club and an English club. He won the European Cup Winners' Cup with Aberdeen and the European Cup Winners' Cup and the European Champions' Cup with Manchester United.

- **By the end of the 2002/03 season** Alex Ferguson had guided Manchester United to eight Premier League titles, two European trophies, four FA Cups and one Football League Cup.

- **By the start of the 2003/04 season** only three different managers had guided teams to Premiership title: Alex Ferguson at Manchester United, Arsene Wenger at Arsenal and Kenny Dalglish at Blackburn Rovers.

- **At the start of the 2003/04 season** Chris Coleman at 33 was the Premiership's youngest manager and Bobby Robson at 70 was the oldest.

- **In September 2003** Glenn Hoddle became the first managerial casualty of the 2003/04 Premiership season when he was sacked as boss of Tottenham.

What's in a nickname?

▲ *Reading's team were known as the Biscuitmen.*

- **Reading were originally nicknamed the Biscuitmen** due to the main trade in the town. In 1970 their nickname was changed to the Royals due to their location in the Royal County of Berkshire.

- **Sheffield United** are nicknamed the Blades to reflect the city's historic links with the production of cutlery.

- **Arsenal are nicknamed the Gunners** due to their connection in the 19th century with the Royal Arsenal, an important munitions factory.

- **York City are nicknamed the Minstermen** and are the only club in the Football League that are named after a building – York Minster.

- **In 2002 Posh Spice aka Victoria Beckham**, attempted to prevent Peterborough from registering their nickname of The Posh as a trademark.

- **Southampton are nicknamed the Saints** after the former name of the club Southampton St Marys.

▶ *The Hatters is the nickname given to Luton Town's team.*

- **Luton Town are nicknamed the Hatters** as the town was once famous for its hat manufacturers.

- **In the 1960s George Best** acquired the nickname of the 5th Beatle due to his long hair, playboy lifestyle and fanatical adulation usually reserved for pop stars.

- **Plymouth Argyle are nicknamed the Pilgrims** as the Pilgrim Fathers sailed from Plymouth on their historic 1620 voyage to America onboard *The Mayflower*.

- **Everton are nicknamed the Toffees** after a 19th-century shop called Mother Nobletts Toffee Shop that stood close to their Goodison Park ground.

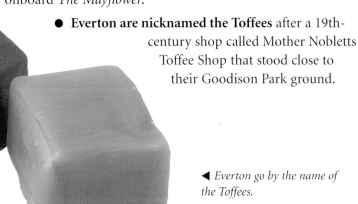

◀ *Everton go by the name of the Toffees.*

13

Around the grounds

▲ *Demolition work gets underway at Wembley Stadium, London, where a new 90,000-seat stadium is scheduled to open in 2006.*

- **During World War II** Old Trafford was destroyed in bombing raids, and as a result Manchester United played their home games at Maine Road until 1949.

- **In 1981 Loftus Road**, the home of Queen's Park Rangers, became the first ground in the Football League to install an artificial pitch.

- **The first British football club** to install an all-seater stadium was Aberdeen.

- **Aberdeen's stadium is called Pittodrie**, a name that derives from the Pict language and actually means, 'heap of dung'.

- **The two nearest grounds to each other in the Football League** are Nottingham Forest's City Ground and Notts County's Meadow Lane that lie on either side of the River Trent.

▶ *The world-famous landmark of the Wembley Stadium's twin towers is dismantled.*

- **The Nou Camp Stadium**, home of Barcelona, has a capacity of 110,000 that is limited to 100,000 by FIFA rules. The Spanish giants boast an incredible 92,000 season ticket holders.

- **In 1950 the Maracana Stadium in Rio de Janeiro** hosted the World Cup final in front of a world record crowd of 199,854.

- **On April 26, 1923 Wembley Stadium hosted its first game**, the FA Cup final between Bolton and West Ham. In 2000 Germany beat England 1–0 in the last game at Wembley before its demolition.

- **In 1994 the Pontiac Silverdome in Detroit** was the venue of the first-ever World Cup match to be played indoors.

- **Clubs that have moved grounds in recent years** include Derby County from the Baseball Ground to Pride Park, Sunderland from Roker Park to the Stadium of Light and Manchester City from Maine Road to the City of Manchester Stadium.

Bend it like Beckham

- **David Robert Joseph Beckham** was born on May 2, 1975 in Leytonstone, London.

- **As a starry-eyed youngster** David Beckham turned up for a trial at Tottenham Hotspur wearing a Manchester United football kit.

- **As an 11 year old, David was crowned** TSB Bobby Charlton Soccer Skills Champion for his age group.

- **When David was 12 years old** he represented Manchester United as the clubs mascot when the team played West Ham at Upton Park.

- **Beckham signed for Manchester United** as a trainee on July 8, 1991 and was part of the famous 1992 Youth Cup winning team that included Ryan Giggs, Paul Scholes and the Neville brothers in their ranks.

- **David Beckham made his Football League debut** in the 1994/95 season, playing for Preston North End during a loan spell from Manchester United.

- **David made his Premier League debut playing for Manchester United** against Leeds on April 2, 1995 and went on to become part of the historic treble winning team of 1999.

- **Beckham won his first international cap for England** on September 1, 1996 against Moldova and captained his country for the first time in November 2000 against Italy.

- **David announced his intention of marrying Victoria Adams** after spotting her in a Spice Girls video. They eventually tied the knot in July 1999 with his Manchester United team mate Gary Neville as best man.

● **In June 2003 David Beckham joined the Spanish club Real Madrid** for a fee of £24.5 million.

▼ David Beckham (right) celebrates his goal against Malaga with Real Madrid team-mate Michel Salgado.

Football transfers

- **In 1905 Alf Common became the first footballer** to be transferred for £1000 when Middlesbrough signed him from their local rivals, Sunderland.

- **In 1928 David Jack** became the first footballer to be transferred for £10,000 when Arsenal signed him from Bolton Wanderers.

- **Denis Law was the first British footballer** to be transferred for a fee of £100,000 when Manchester United signed him from the Italian club Torino in 1962.

- **In 1961 Jimmy Greaves moved from AC Milan to Tottenham** for a fee of £99,999 as he did not want to become the first £100,000 footballer.

- **In 1970 Martin Peters became the first British footballer** to be transferred for £200,000 when he moved from West Ham to Tottenham Hotspur.

- **The first British footballer to be involved in a £1 million transfer** was Trevor Francis who moved from Birmingham to Nottingham Forest in 1979.

- **Nigel Martin was the first British goalkeeper** to be sold for a fee of £1 million when he moved to Crystal Palace from Bristol Rovers in 1989.

- **Paul Gascoine was the first British player** to be sold for a fee of £2 million on his move from Newcastle to Tottenham in 1988.

- **In 1994 Chris Sutton became the first British player** to be sold for £5 million when he moved from Norwich City to Blackburn Rovers.

- **The first British player to be sold for a fee in excess of £10 million** was Alan Shearer when he moved from Blackburn to Newcastle in 1996 for an actual fee of £15 million.

▶ *Denis Law was known as The King. Here he is seen in action at Manchester in 1968.*

Foreign football

▲ *Milan's defender Maldini (right) vies with Juventus players Legrotallie, Nedved and Appiah at San Siro Staduim in Milan in 2003.*

- **The famed black-and-white striped shirt** worn by Juventus was adopted in 1903 after the Italian club borrowed a football kit from the English league club, Notts County.

- **The African Nations Cup** was first contested in 1957 with Egypt winning the inaugural trophy. Egypt went on to lift the trophy a further three times, a record bettered only by Ghana with five wins.

- **The South American equivalent of the European Champions Cup** is called the Copa Libertadores. It was first contested in 1960 and the first winners were the Uruguayan club Penarol.

- **Italy's equivalent to the Premiership division** is called Serie A, Germany's equivalent is called the Bundesliga and Spain's equivalent is called La Liga.

- **The Bundesliga was founded in Germany in 1963** and by 2003 its most successful team was Bayern Munich with a total of 13 championships.

- **Despite never winning the championship in England's top division** Bobby Robson won the Dutch league title with PSV Eindhoven and the Portuguese league title with FC Porto.

- **In the 1990s three Brazilian footballers** were voted World Footballer of the Year – Romario, Rivaldo and Ronaldo (twice).

- **In 1990 Italian clubs won the three major European trophies.** Sampdoria won the European Cup Winners' Cup, Juventus won the UEFA Cup and AC Milan won the European Champions' Cup.

- **In 1993 the French club Marseilles** won the European Champions' Cup but were subsequently stripped of the title when the club president Bernard Tapie was implicated in a bribery scandal.

- **On December 11, 2000** FIFA presented the Spanish club Real Madrid with the Club of the Century Award.

The FA Cup

◀ Manchester United's Teddy Sheringham (right) and David Beckham celebrate the first goal scored at the 1999 FA Cup final at Wembley.

● **The first FA Cup final** in 1872 at the Kennington Oval saw the Wanderers beat the Royal Engineers 1–0 to lift the trophy.

● **The 15 teams that contested the first FA Cup competition** were the Wanderers, the Royal Engineers, Barnes, Civil Service, Clapham Rovers, Crystal Palace, Donington School, Great Marlow, Hampstead Heathens, Harrow Chequers, Hitchin, Maidenhead, Queen's Park, Reigate Priory and Upton Park.

- **In 1901 Tottenham Hotspur** became the first and only non-league team to win the FA Cup. They collected the trophy as a member of the Southern League beating Sheffield United 3–1 in the final.

- **The only non-English team** to lift the Cup is Cardiff City who beat Arsenal 1–0 in the 1927 final.

- **Shirt numbers were seen for the first time in the FA Cup final in 1933**, which saw Everton beat Manchester City 3-0. Everton wore numbers 1 to 11 and City wore numbers 12 to 22.

- **To date the only man to score a hat-trick** in an FA Cup final is Stanley Mortensen in Blackpool's 4–3 defeat of Bolton in the 1953 final.

- **The 12 different stadiums** to have hosted the FA Cup final are Kennington Oval, Bramall Lane, Fallowfield, Lillie Bridge, Crystal Palace, Old Trafford, Stamford Bridge, Goodison Park, The Baseball Ground, Burnden Park, Wembley and The Millennium Stadium.

- **Two pairs of brothers have helped Manchester United** win the FA Cup: Brian and Jimmy Greenhoff in 1977 and Phil and Gary Neville in 1996.

- **The fastest goal scored in a Wembley FA Cup final** came in 1997. Roberto di Matteo scored for Chelsea against Middlesbrough in 42 seconds.

> **FASCINATING FACT**
> In 1999 Manchester United became the first club to win the trophy for the 10th time.

The European Champions' Cup

- **The competition was the brainchild** of a French journalist called Gabriel Hanot who invited 16 teams to take part in a knock-out cup tournament, first contested in 1956.

- **The first five tournaments** were all won by Real Madrid and by 2002 the Spanish club had collected the trophy a record nine times.

- **The individual scoring record for the Champions' Cup** is held by Alfredo di Stefano, who scored 49 goals in 58 matches for Real Madrid in the 1950s and 1960s.

- **The only three clubs to have won the cup** in three consecutive seasons are Real Madrid 1956 to 1960, Ajax 1971 to 1973 and Bayern Munich 1974 to 1976.

- **The only British clubs to have lifted the trophy are** Celtic, Manchester United, Liverpool, Nottingham Forest and Aston Villa.

- **In 1982 Aston Villa** were crowned European champions despite only finishing 12th in their own domestic league that year.

- **In 1997 and 1998 Juventus** became the first club to be beaten in the final in consecutive years, losing out to Borussia Dortmund and Real Madrid.

- **The final has been contested by teams** from the same country on just two occasions. In the 2000 final Real Madrid beat Valencia 3–0 and in 2003 AC Milan beat Juventus on a penalty shoot-out.

- **For the 2003/04 competition** the top eight seeded teams were AC Milan, Real Madrid, Manchester United, Bayern Munich, Lazio, Arsenal, Juventus and Deportiva La Coruna.

▲ *A scene from the European Champions' Cup final in May 1957. Real Madrid beat Fiorentina 2–0.*

25

England internationals

▲ *Bobby Moore is held aloft by his team-mates after England won the World Cup in 1966 beating Germany 4–2 in extra time.*

- **The first official international fixture** in world football saw England draw 0–0 with Scotland on November 30, 1872.

- **England's biggest win in an international match** was a 13–0 demolition of Ireland in 1882. Their heaviest defeat was a 7–1 drubbing at the hands of Hungary in 1954.

- **Billy Wright was the first player to win 100 international caps** for England. The only other players to exceed a century of caps are Bobby Moore, Bobby Charlton and Peter Shilton.

- **The first foreign team to beat England at Wembley** were Hungary who recorded a 6–3 victory in 1953.

- **The oldest player to make his England debut is Leslie Compton**, who in 1950 won his first England cap at the age of 38.

▲ *England's Wayne Rooney celebrates after making it 2–0 against Leichtenstein during a Euro 2004 qualifier.*

- **The record for captaining England** is jointly held by Bobby Moore and Billy Wright, who both skippered England on 90 occasions.

- **Brian Robson scored the fastest-ever international goal** for England, notching after just 27 seconds in a 1982 World Cup match against France.

- **On February 12, 2003** Wayne Rooney at the age of 17 years and 111 days became the youngest-ever player to be capped for England.

- **In 1978 the Nottingham Forest fullback Viv Anderson** became the first black player to be capped for England.

- **In a 1968 match against Yugoslavia,** Alan Mullery became the first England player to be sent off.

Football milestones

- **The oldest football league club** in Britain is Notts County, founded in 1862.
- **The 12 founder members of the Football League** were Accrington Stanley, Aston Villa, Blackburn Rovers, Bolton Wanderers, Burnley, Derby County, Everton, Notts County, Preston North End, Stoke City, West Brom and Wolves.
- **The first ever penalty kick** was scored by Wolverhampton Wanderers star John Heath against Accrington Stanley in September 1891.
- **The Football League was founded in 1888** and the first winners of the championship were Preston North End.
- **In 1891 the goal net was introduced.** It was invented by a Liverpudlian called John Alexander Brodie who designed a huge pocket for the goal to remove any arguments as to whether a goal had been scored or not.
- **In 1950** the use of a white football was legalized.
- **In January 1974**, Millwall faced Fulham in the first-ever league game to be contested on a Sunday.
- **In 1981 the Football League introduced** the three points for a win ruling in an attempt to create more attacking football.
- **The first women's World Cup** was held in China in 1991 with the USA winning the tournament.
- **In 1928 Arsenal became the first British football club** to wear numbers on their shirts.

▲ *Sweden's Malin Mostroem (right) drives past German defenders during the 2003 FIFA Women's World Cup final in 2003.*

British hall of fame

- **Dixie Dean** – Dixie was the only player to score 60 goals in one season and notched 349 goals in 399 games for Everton, all for the princely sum of £8 per week.

- **Stanley Matthews** – Nicknamed 'The Wizard of Dribble', Stanley Matthews at 42 is the oldest-ever player to be capped for England and was also the first footballer to receive a knighthood.

- **Bobby Charlton** – Known for his powerful shooting ability Bobby Charlton scored a record 49 goals for England in 106 matches and received a knighthood in 1994.

- **Bobby Moore** – At 22 Moore is the youngest-ever player to captain England. He led England to World Cup glory in 1966 and won a total of 108 caps before his life was tragically cut short by cancer at the age of 51.

- **Geoff Hurst** – Geoff Hurst was knighted in 1998, 32 years after scoring a hat-trick in the World Cup final.

- **George Best** – Best is the only Irishman to be voted European Footballer of the Year and the legendary Pele once described Best as, 'the world's most gifted player'.

- **Kevin Keegan** – Following humble beginnings at Scunthorpe United, Keegan battled his way to the top and was twice voted European Footballer of the Year.

- **Bryan Robson** – Robson won 90 international caps, 65 as captain. His sterling leadership of England earned him the nickname 'Captain Marvel'.

- **Alan Shearer** – The most prolific striker in modern-day British football, he was the first player to score 200 goals in the Premiership. By the end of 2003 he had passed the 250 mark.

- **Michael Owen** – At 18 years of age Michael Owen became the youngest player to score for England at the World Cup finals. In 2001 he was voted European Footballer of the Year.

▶ *English forward Kevin Keegan gets ready to kick the ball during a Football League match in 1981.*

31

World hall of fame

- **Pele** – Nicknamed 'The Black Pearl', Pele is considered by many to be the greatest-ever footballer. He played in four World Cups for Brazil winning three, and scored two goals in the 1958 final aged 17.

- **Franz Beckenbauer** – Nicknamed 'The Kaiser', Beckenbauer is the only person to have captained and managed a World Cup winning team, collecting the trophy with Germany in 1974 and 1990.

- **Michael Platini** – Platini is the only player to be voted European Footballer of the Year in three consecutive years and went on to become Vice President of the French Football Federation.

- **Zinedine Zidane** – A World Cup winner with France and a European Cup winner with Real Madrid, Zidane became the world's most expensive footballer when Madrid bought him from Juventus for £45.62 million.

- **Ronaldo** – The Brazilian superstar made his international debut aged just 17 and was a World Cup winner in 2002. To date he is the only player to be voted World Footballer of the Year on three occasions.

- **Ferenc Puskas** – Puskas scored 83 goals in 84 internationals for Hungary and as one of the many stars of Real Madrid he is the only player to score four fair goals in the European Cup final.

- **Gerd Muller** – Nicknamed 'Der Bomber', Muller holds the goal-scoring record for World Cup finals, with a total of 14 goals scored in the 1970 and 1974 tournaments.

▶ *Diego Maradona (right) in action in the 1968 World Cup quarterfinal match between Argentina and England.*

- **Diego Maradona** – Maradona almost single-handedly guided Argentina to World Cup glory in 1986. His infamous 'hand of God goal' against England was followed by an individual effort considered to be one of the greatest-ever goals scored at the World Cup.

- **Johann Cruyff** – The Dutch maestro was voted European Footballer of the Year on three occasions and went on to become a successful manager at Ajax and Barcelona.

. . . FASCINATING FACT . . .
Eusebio da Silva Ferreira was the star of the 1966 World Cup and was the leading scorer in the tournament with nine goals.

Rules of the game

- **The referee's whistle** was first used in 1878. Prior to its introduction the men in the middle waved a handkerchief to attract the players' attention.

- **The rules state that the field of play** must be rectangular and have a minimum width of 45 m and a minimum length of 90 m.

- **The width of goalposts must not exceed 12 cm.** The distance between the posts is 7.32 m with the height of the crossbar being 2.44 m.

▲ *A whistle is an essential part of the football referee's equipment.*

- **If the ball passes directly into the net** from a throw-in without touching another player then a goal kick is awarded.

- **In July 2000 a new rule was introduced** stating that if goalkeepers held onto the ball for longer than six seconds a free kick was awarded to the opponents. This replaced the old ruling allowing keepers to take no more than four steps whilst holding the ball.

- **A recent addition to the rules** allows goalkeepers to move along their goal line when facing a penalty kick. However, should they move forward of the line the penalty should be retaken if it is missed.

- **If the ball strikes the referee and goes into the net** a goal is awarded as the referee is considered to be part of the field of play.

▶ *Belgrade's midfielder Delibasic (right) is given a red card by Italian referee Messina in a 2003 Champions' League match.*

● **Red and yellow cards** were first used in the World Cup in 1970 and although numerous yellow cards were shown at the tournament not a single red card was brandished.

● **Goalkeepers are not allowed to handle the ball** from a deliberate back pass kicked by the foot. If any other part of the body is used when making the back pass the keeper may then handle the ball.

● **A new ruling states** that 30 seconds of added time should be allowed for each substitution and each goal scored in any of the 45 minute halves.

35

The World Cup

- **The first trophy** contested in the World Cup was called the Jules Rimet Trophy and was named after the FIFA president who organized the first tournament.

- **In 1930 France and Mexico** played in the first-ever World Cup match with France winning the game 4–1.

- **Brazil were allowed to keep the first World Cup trophy** in 1970 after becoming the first nation to win the tournament on three occasions.

- **Brazil is the only country** to have played in every single World Cup final.

- **The 1958 World Cup** in Sweden marked the only occasion when England, Scotland, Wales and Northern Ireland all qualified for the final stages.

- **The most goals scored** in the final stages of a World Cup match is 12, in the 1954 quarterfinal that saw Austria beat Switzerland 7–5.

- **Jaiirzinho is the only player** to score in every round of a World Cup final, achieving his feat with Brazil in 1970.

- **In 1982 Norman Whiteside** of Northern Ireland became the youngest-ever footballer to play in the World Cup final shortly after celebrating his 17th birthday.

- **Jose Batista of Uruguay** is the holder of an unwanted record of being the fastest-ever recipient of a red card in a World Cup game. He received his marching orders after just 56 seconds in a 1986 group game against Scotland.

- **In 1998 the French star Laurent Blanc** became scorer of the World Cup's first ever Golden Goal, hitting the net in the 113th minute in a second round match against Paraguay.

▲ *Northern Ireland's forward Norman Whiteside (right) fights for the ball with Austrian Bruno Pezzey during the World Cup final in 1982.*

Strange but true

- **In 1875 a wooden crossbar** was added to the goalposts. Previously a piece of tape had been used.

- **In September 1955**, Hibernian FC became the first British club to compete in the European Cup.

- **In 1966 Queen Elizabeth II** named one of her race horses *Charlton* in honour of the World Cup winning brothers Bobby and Jack Charlton.

- **A 1969 World Cup qualifying match** between Honduras and El Salvador witnessed massed rioting amongst the spectators and eventually sparked a war between the two opposing nations.

- **The only four league teams** in England and Scotland with the letters ABCD and E in their names are Cambridge United, Wycombe Wanderers, Clydebank and Cowdenbeath.

- **Paulo Rossi returned to playing football** just two weeks before the start of the 1982 World Cup after being suspended for two years for his involvement in a bribery scandal. Rossi went on to become the top scorer at the tournament in helping Italy to win the trophy.

- **The 20 players who made up Bulgaria's Euro 96 squad** all had names ending with the letter V including Popov, Ivanov and Donkov.

- **Manchester United star Ryan Giggs** represents Wales at full international level despite playing for England's schoolboys as a teenager under the name of Ryan Wilson.

- **In the 2001/02 season** Chelsea became the first Premiership club to field a team comprising of 11 foreign players.

- **On September 13, 2003** York City played Yeovil Town, the first time two teams beginning with Y had played each other in the Football League.

▲ *Bulgaria's Hristo Stoitchkov plays against Spain's Rafael Alkorta (left) in the European Football Championships in 1996. All members of the Bulgarian team had surnames ending with V.*

Index